You Can Draw

Boats

By Mark Bergin

SALARIYA

Published in Great Britain in MMXII by
Book House, an imprint of
The Salariya Book Company Ltd
25 Marlborough Place, Brighton BN1 1UB

1 3 5 7 9 8 6 4 2

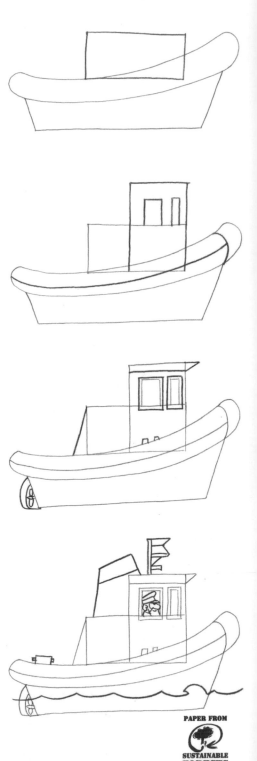

Please visit our websites at **www.salariya.com** or
www.book-house.co.uk for **free** electronic versions of:
You Wouldn't Want to Be an Egyptian Mummy!
You Wouldn't Want to Be a Roman Gladiator!
You Wouldn't Want to be a Polar Explorer!
**You Wouldn't Want to Sail on a 19th-Century
　　　　Whaling Ship!**

Author: Mark Bergin was born in Hastings in 1961. He
studied at Eastbourne College of Art and has specialised
in historical reconstructions as well as aviation and
maritime subjects since 1983. He lives in Bexhill-on-
Sea with his wife and three children.

Editor: Rob Walker

PB ISBN: 978-1-908759-57-3

A CIP catalogue record for this book is available from
the British Library.

Printed and bound in China.
Printed on paper from sustainable sources.

Visit our **new** online shop at
shop.salariya.com
for great offers, gift ideas, all our new releases

and free postage and packaging.

PAPER FROM
SUSTAINABLE
FORESTS

Contents

Introduction

Learning to draw is fun. In this book a finished drawing will be broken up into stages as a guide to completing your own drawing. However, this is only the beginning. The more you practise, the better you will draw. Have fun coming up with cool designs, adding more incredible details and using new materials to achieve different effects!

This is an example showing how each drawing will be built up in easy stages. New sections of drawing will be shown in colour to make each additional step clear.

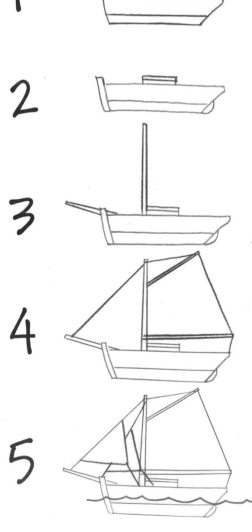

1

2

3

4

5

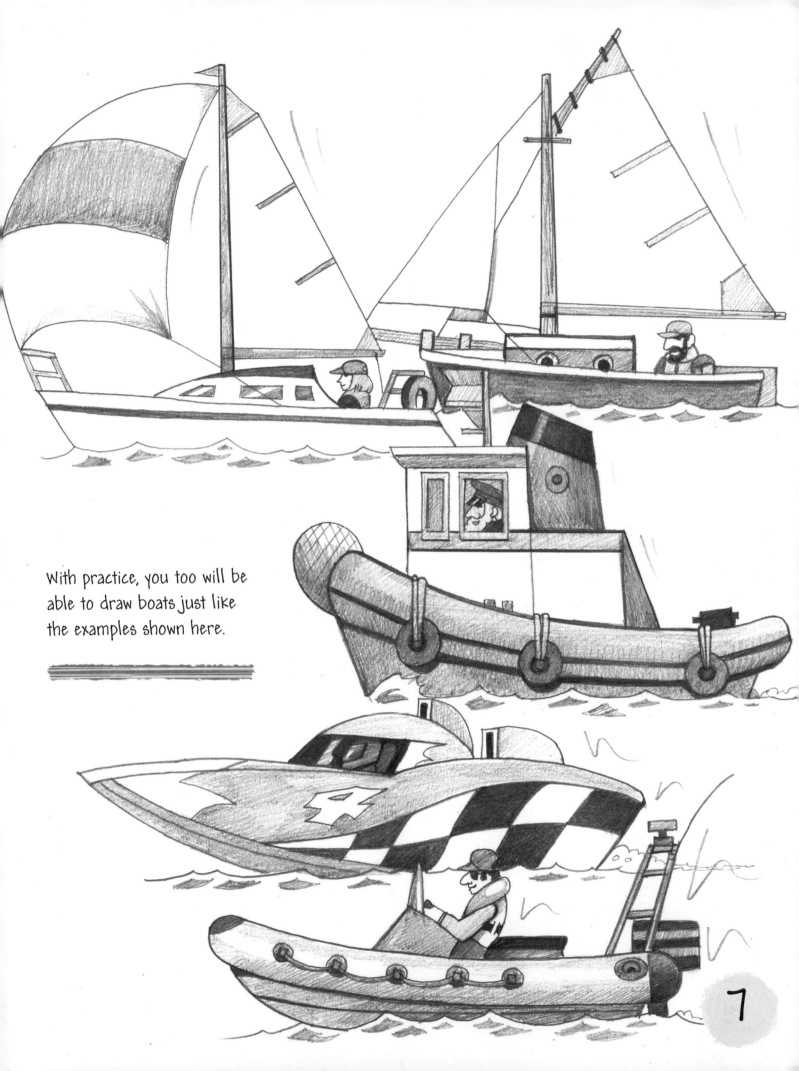

With practice, you too will be able to draw boats just like the examples shown here.

Materials

There are many different art materials available which you can use to draw and colour in your boats. Try out each one for new and exciting results. The more you practise with them, the better your drawing skills will get!

Use a pencil to draw the shape of your boat. Any mistakes you make can easily be erased, as can any construction lines that are left over at the end of your drawing.

An eraser can be used to rub out any pencil mistakes. It can also be used to create highlights on pencil drawings.

You can go over your finished pencil lines with pen to make the lines bolder. But remember, a pen line is permanent so you can't erase any mistakes!

Coloured pencils come in a huge range of colours and can be layered over each other for new and exciting effects.

Pastels can be smudged and blended together to give you all sorts of different colours.

Felt tip pens can add vibrant colour to your drawing. But remember that they are hard to layer and the colour is permanent so you can't erase any mistakes!

9

Inspiration

Many types of boats are made throughout the world. You can choose any of them as the inspiration for your cartoon-style drawing. Looking at photos, magazines or books can give you new ideas and new designs to try.

When turning your boat into a cartoon-style, two-dimensional drawing, concentrate on the key elements you want to include and the overall shape of the boat.

One way to make your boat look cool is to exaggerate its key features and perhaps add new ones!

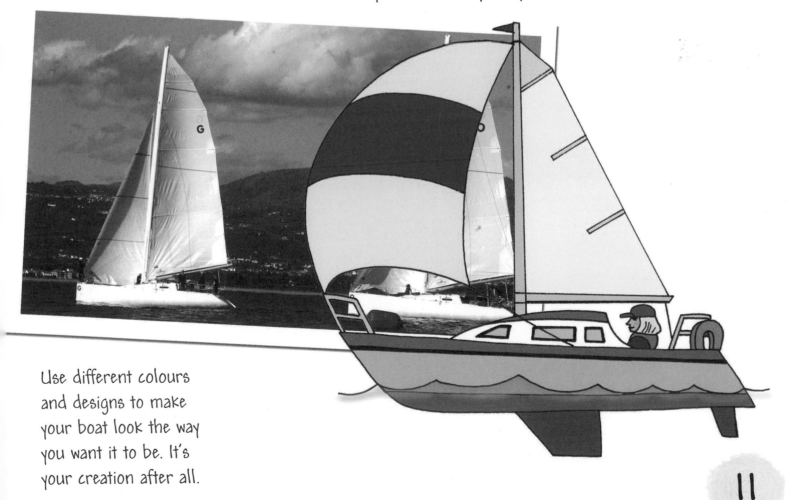

Use different colours and designs to make your boat look the way you want it to be. It's your creation after all.

Laser

The Laser dinghy is a small sailing boat usually piloted by one person. It is used for leisure and racing and in 1996 it became an Olympic class boat.

Start by drawing in the shape of the hull. Draw a line through it.

Add another line higher up and draw in the centreboard.

Draw in the mast using curved lines and then add the shape of the sail.

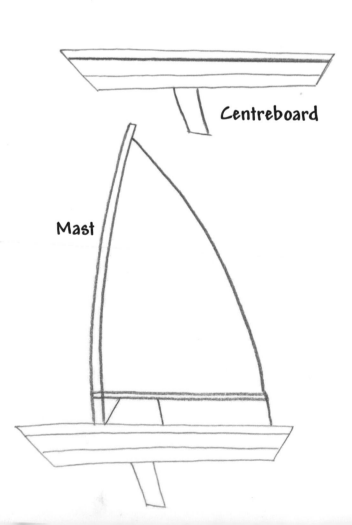

Centreboard

Mast

Add more detail to the sail
and draw in the rudder.

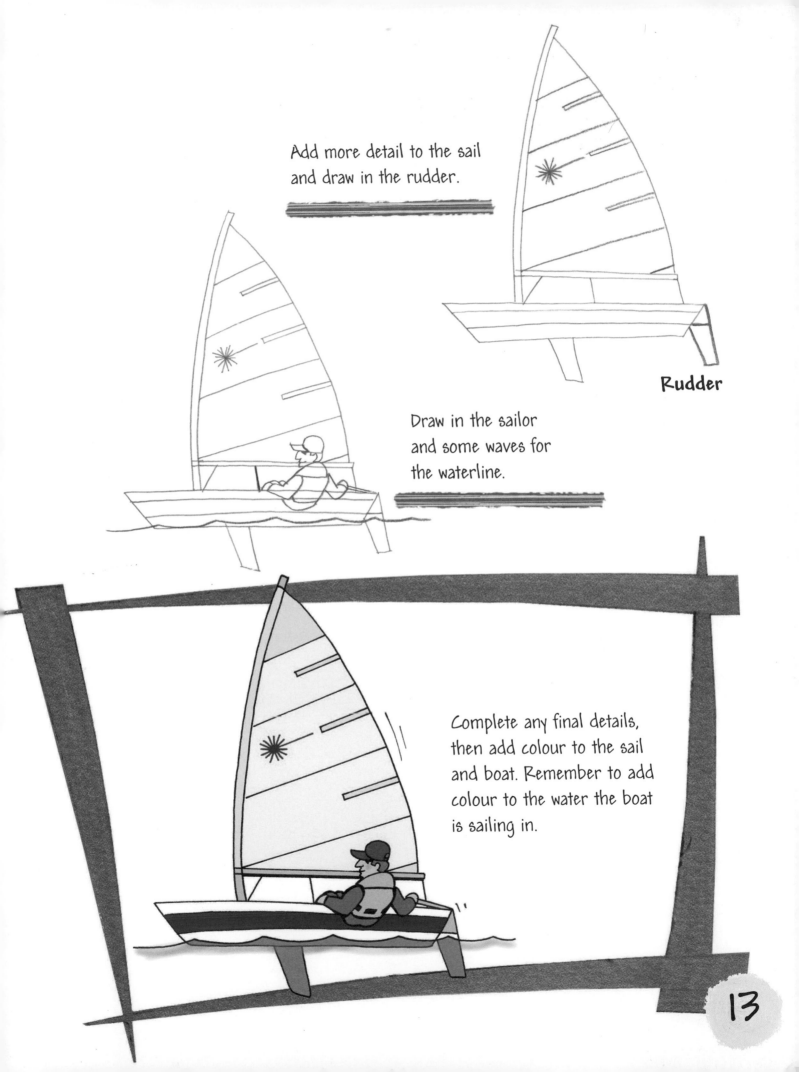

Rudder

Draw in the sailor
and some waves for
the waterline.

Complete any final details,
then add colour to the sail
and boat. Remember to add
colour to the water the boat
is sailing in.

Racing boat

These high-performance racing boats are specially designed to move across the water at high speeds and take part in very exciting races.

Start by drawing in the shape of the hull.

Extend the hull at the rear. Add a line along the top of the hull.

Draw in a curved line on the underside of the hull. Add the small, domed cockpit.

Add another curved line to the base of the hull and a window to the cockpit. Draw in the large engine air intakes.

Engine intakes

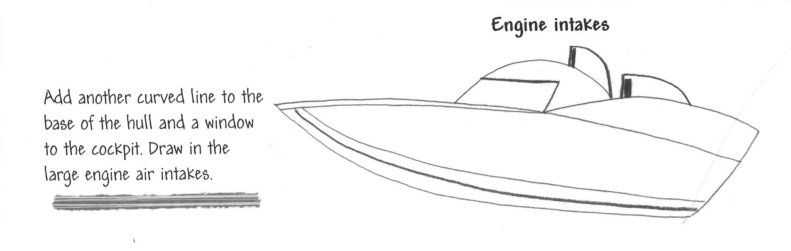

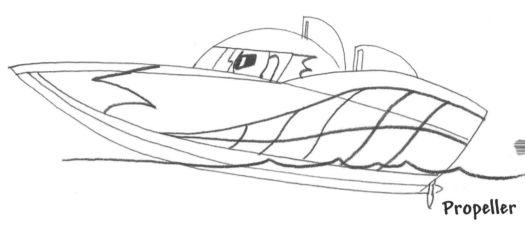

Draw in the driver and the paintwork designs. Add in the wavy waterline and a propeller.

Propeller

Complete all the remaining details and add colour to your drawing. Remember everything below the waterline should be coloured in blue!

US coast guard

The coast guard boat has to be fast and durable in all weather conditions to mount rescues and police the shores.

Start by drawing in the shape of the hull.

Draw in the cabin shape rising above the hull.

Bridge

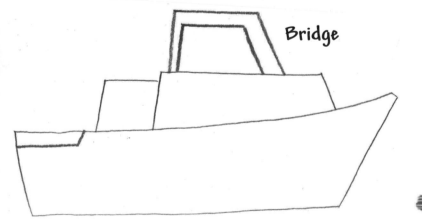

Draw in the bridge with a window. Add extra detail at the rear of the hull.

Draw in a propeller. Add the paintwork design and more detail on the window.

Propeller

Radar

Light

Add the pilot and draw in an aerial, radar and light. Add more detail to the cabin. Draw in the waterline.

○ 47

Complete your drawing by finishing any remaining details and then colour in the different sections of the boat.

Power boat

This power boat can be used out at sea for pleasure cruises or even for sports like fishing or diving.

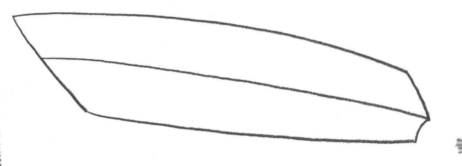

Start by drawing in the shape of the hull. Add a line through the middle.

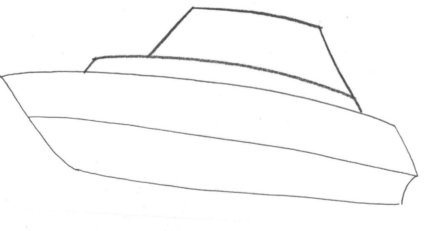

Add the cabin shape and the bridge.

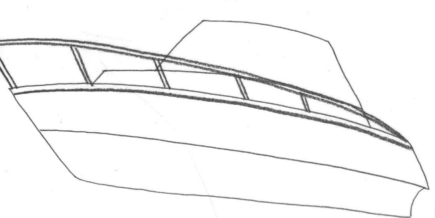

Add a railing on top of the hull.

Draw in a window in the bridge and portholes round the hull. Add two lines on the lower part of the hull.

Radar

Draw in the pilot and the radar. Add the waterline and a propeller.

Complete your drawing by adding any remaining detail, then colour it in.

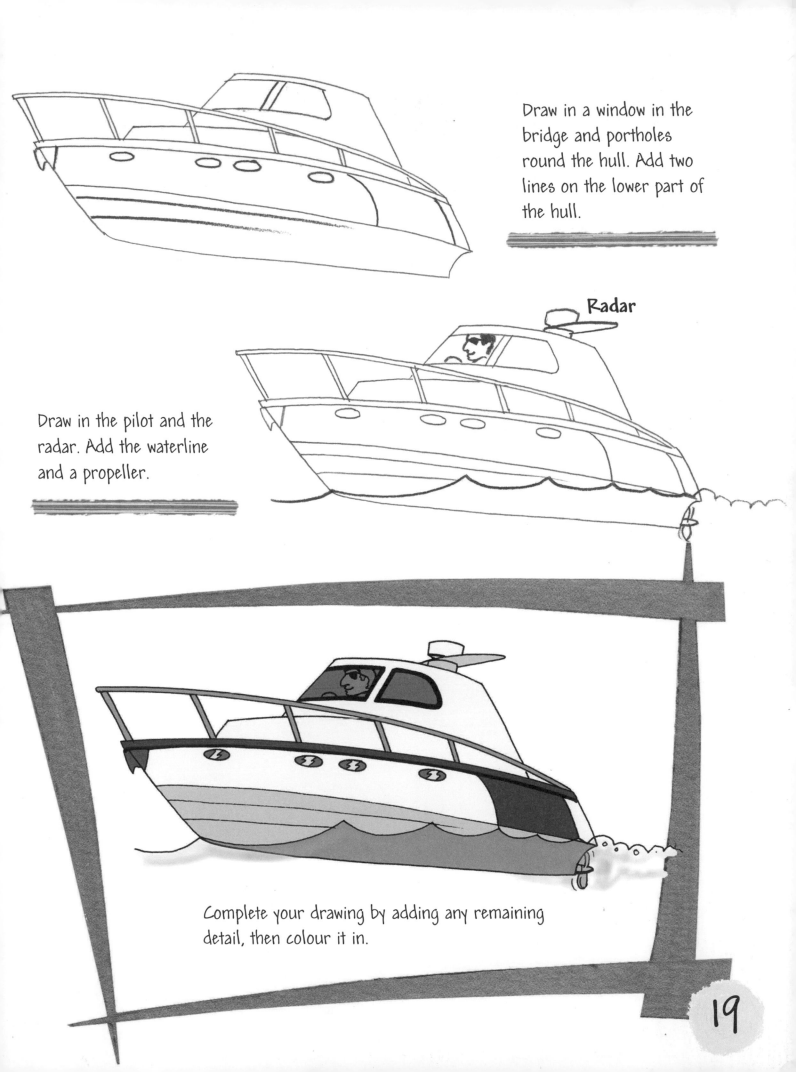

RHIB

A rigid-hulled inflatable boat (RHIB) is a lightweight boat which is designed to adapt to all weather conditions.

Start by drawing in the two sections of the hull.

Draw in the control panel and window.

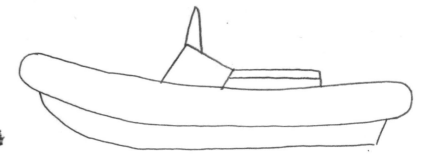

Draw in the ropes along the top section of the hull. Add an outboard motor at the rear.

Outboard motor

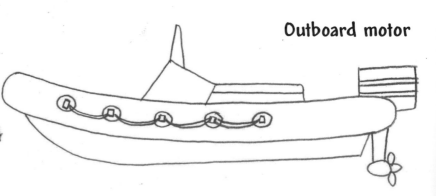

Draw a line through the lower part of the hull and add some small details. Draw in the framework at the rear of the boat and add an aerial and radar.

Radar

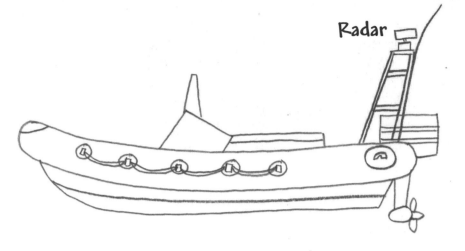

Draw in the pilot at the controls and add the waterline.

Complete all the remaining details, then colour in the different sections of the boat.

Sailing boat

This classic sailing boat harnesses the power of the wind in its sails to propel it forward.

Start by drawing in the shape of the hull.

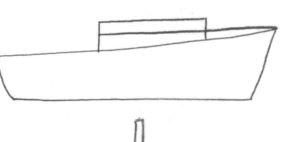

Add the cabin shape.

Mast

Bowsprit

Draw in the mast and the bowsprit. Add a curved line along the top of the hull.

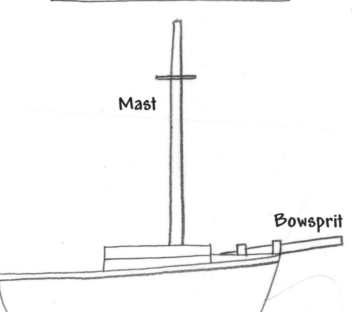

Add two lines between the mast and the bowsprit. Then draw in the boom and add the sails.

Boom

Add the pilot, a rudder and the cabin portholes. Draw in the waterline.

Finish off your drawing by colouring it in and adding any small design details.

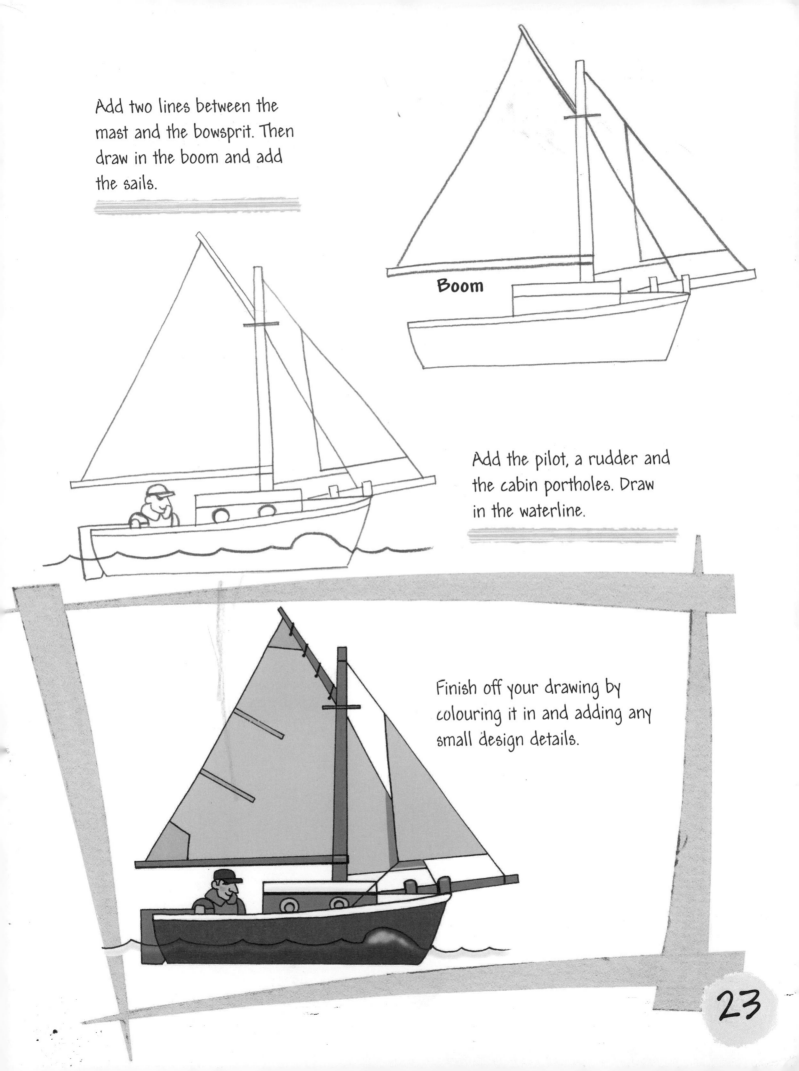

Tug boat

A tug boat is a small, powerful vessel that is used to guide bigger boats in and out of harbours by towing or pushing them.

Start by drawing in the two sections of the hull.

Add a rectangle for the main structure of the boat.

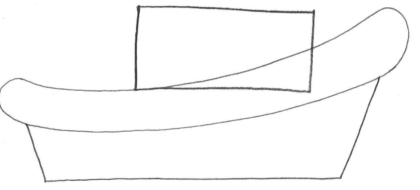

Draw an upright rectangle for the bridge and add windows. Add detail to the top part of the hull.

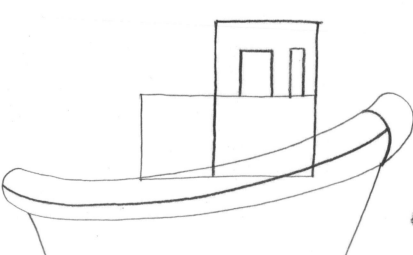

Draw in the roof and windows of the bridge. Add some details to the main structure and draw in a propeller.

Radar

Funnel

Draw in a funnel and add the radar structure. Add the pilot and the extra detail at the rear. Draw in the waterline.

Finish off your drawing by completing all the small details and adding colour to each section. Add puffs of smoke to the funnel.

Fishing boat

This boat is used for the sport of ocean fishing. The rods at the rear are used to try to catch large fish or even sharks!

Start by drawing in the shape of the hull.

Draw in the cabin and bridge above it.

Draw in a front railing and add a window to the cabin. Add a line to the hull.

Draw in the small details near the bow and the waterline. Add a propeller and rear platform.

Bow

Propeller

Draw in a large 'X' shaped frame with a roof. Add the pilot and three fishing rods.

Complete your drawing by adding all the remaining details and colouring it in.

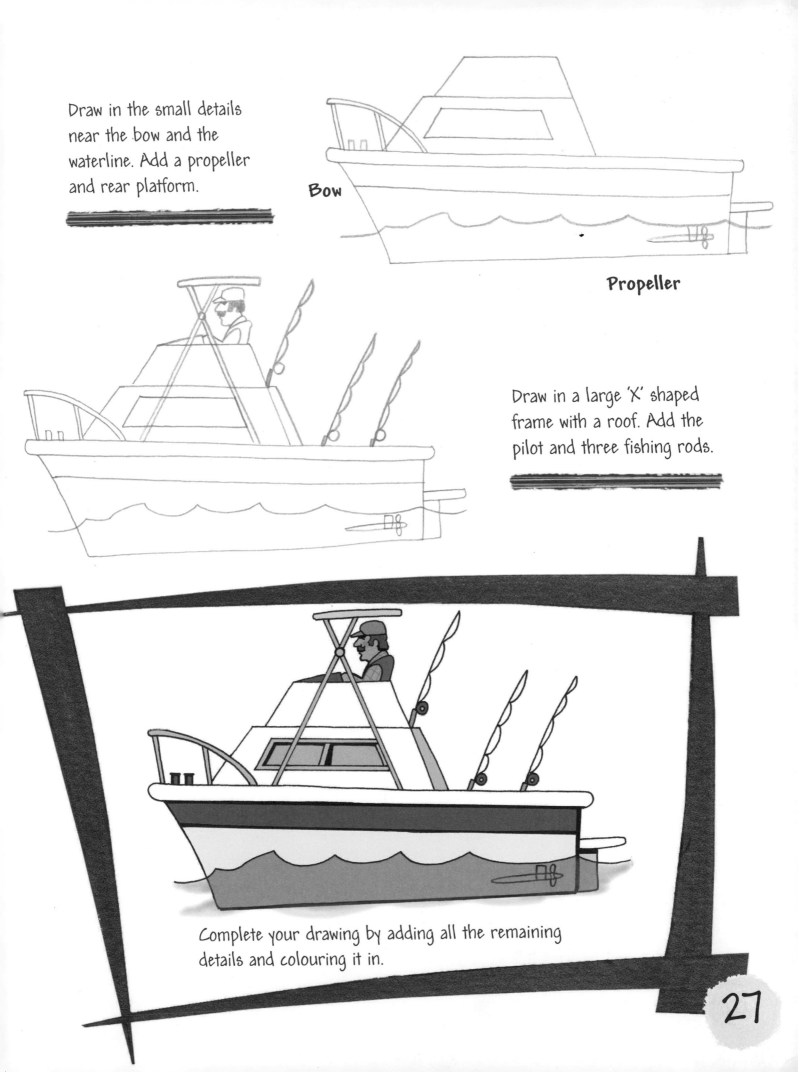

Yacht

This yacht can be used purely for pleasure sailing or for small journeys.

Start by drawing the shape of the hull. Add a line along the top edge.

Draw in the cabin and add another line to the hull. Draw in the fin keel underneath the hull.

Fin Keel

Mast

Draw in the mast and the rudder.

Rudder

Draw in railings at the bow
and stern. Add the boom to
the mast and draw in the sails.
Add windows to the cabin.

Boom

Add a billowing sail at the
bow and draw in the pilot.
Add the waterline.

Colour in the different
sections of your yacht.
Add any extra design
details you wish.

More views

For an extra challenge try drawing your boats from the front or rear! Practising different views will help you improve your drawing.

Front View

Yacht

Start with the hull of the boat.

Add the main structure and the waterline.

Draw in the mast and a sail.

Draw in another sail and a window.

Back View

Start by drawing in the shape of the hull.

Draw in the main structure. Add propellers and a rudder to the hull.

Add the bridge and draw in the waterline.

Draw in windows, aerials, a door and a radar. Add the side rails and two dots above the waterline.

Tug boat

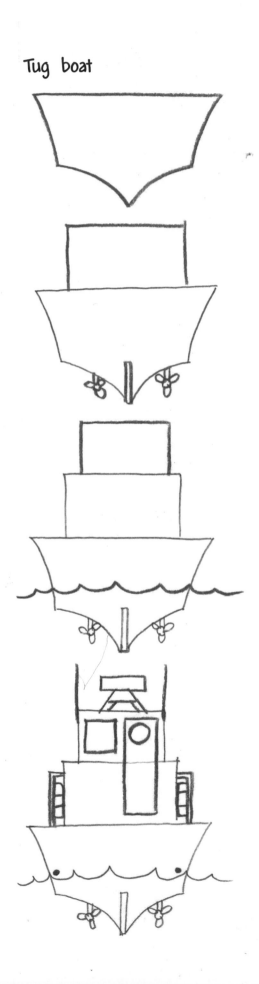

Glossary

boom A long pole used especially to stretch the bottom of a sail.

bow The front of a boat or ship.

bowsprit A large pole for sails sticking out from the bow of a ship.

cockpit An open space in the deck from which a small boat is steered.

dinghy A small rowboat or sailboat; especially one carried on a larger boat.

hull The main body of a boat or ship.

keel A timber or plate running lengthwise along the centre of the bottom of a boat and usually sticking out from the bottom.

mast A long pole that rises from the bottom of a ship or boat and supports the sails.

rudder The hinged flap at the stern of a boat that is used to steer it.

sail A sheet of fabric used to catch wind to move a craft through water or over ice.

stern The rear of a boat or ship.

Index